SURVIVING DIVORCE
IN CALIFORNIA

Expert Answers to Common Questions

By Vincent W. Davis, Esq.

ISBN-13: 978-1500983277
ISBN-10: 1500983276

DISCLAIMER

This publication is intended to be informational only. No legal advice is being given, and no attorney-client relationship is intended to be created by reading this material. If you are facing legal issues, whether criminal or civil, seek professional legal counsel to get your questions answered.

Law Offices of Vincent W. Davis & Associates

150 N. Santa Anita Ave., Ste. 200
Arcadia, CA 91006

(888) 888-6582

Offices in:

Arcadia	Beverly Hills	Irvine
La Mirada	Long Beach	Los Angeles
Ontario	Riverside	Woodland Hills

www.VincentWDavis.com

CLIENT TESTIMONIALS

"Mr. Davis and his team handled two cases for me. My divorce, which involved DCFS, as well as the state welfare office. Both claims were unfounded and a constant battle. Mr. Davis and the other staff members I worked with, throughout the more than year case(s), were outstanding. They had compassion and understanding for the situation and worked diligently to find a way to get the results that I needed. I would highly recommend Mr. Davis and his staff."
Tawnya

....

"Attorney Davis is the best. He met my legal issues and concerns. I will recommend him to my family and friends. He was extremely caring and understanding. He is a great communicator and explained everything step by step, and never kept me in the dark. He always returned my calls." –
Monica V.

....

"Before my court session started, I was described all the possible outcomes and which outcome I was most likely receiving. Also, my lawyer explained how the court session would play out and made me feel confident, knowledgeable, and comfortable going in. In court, my lawyer was very attentive and got the best possible outcome based on what the penalties could have been. I definitely recommend Vincent Walter Davis as a lawyer."
Andrew

CONTENTS

ATTORNEY INTRODUCTION

Attorney Vincent W.
Davis obtained his
Bachelor of Science
degree in Accounting
from Loyola Marymount
University and his Juris
Doctorate from Loyola
Law School of Southern
California. He has been a

member of the California State Bar since
December 1986.

Mr. Davis is also eligible to practice law before
the United States District Court for the Central
District of California; the United States District
Court of Appeals for the 9th Circuit and the
Supreme Court of the United States.

Mr. Davis acted as both trial and appellate
counsel in the published cases of: Marriage of
David and Martha M., (2006) 140 Cal.App.4th
96 and Papakosmas v. Papakosmas, (2007) 483
F.3d 617.

On January 8, 2008, Mr. Davis received a
diploma from the National Institute for Trial
Advocacy. In 2008, he graduated from the Gerry

Spence Trial Lawyers College, and became a member of the Ranch Club - Trial Lawyers College. He was one of 50 lawyers selected nationwide to live, for 22 days on Gerry Spence's Thunderhead Ranch just outside of Dubois, Wyoming. He is the founder and lead attorney of the Law Offices of Vincent W. Davis & Associates. Since 1986, Mr. Davis' practice covers Juvenile Dependency Law and supporting law areas including: family law, juvenile & adult criminal defense.

Mr. Davis and his associates represent clients with companion issues to Juvenile Dependency such as divorce, child custody and visitation, child support and spousal support, domestic violence, paternity, adoption matters, and division of property.

TYPICAL CLIENTS & MARRIAGE STATISTICS

Interviewer: Is there a typical client that you work with when it comes to divorce?

Vincent Davis: No. My clients vary all over the board. I do have an avatar client though.

Interviewer: An avatar client?

Vincent Davis: Yes.

Interviewer: What is an avatar client?

Vincent Davis: My avatar client is a female. She's educated. She hasn't worked outside of the family home in the relationship. She has been a mother and a provider to the children. She's probably the lower income earner in the relationship.

Usually, her husband is leaving her for a younger woman, the secretary or the nurse at work, and trying to take the family business or trying to steal the family business away from her.

Interviewer: What about marriage statistics? Do you think that over the past 5 years, divorce rates have increased or decreased?

Vincent Davis: I'd say they're about the same: 50% of the people I think is the national average. About 50% or 52% of the people that get married are going to end up in divorce.

Interviewer: How many divorce cases do you think you'll be handling this year alone?

Vincent Davis: Maybe 60.

GENDER DIFFERENCES IN DIVORCE

Interviewer: How do men and women view divorce differently?

Vincent Davis: These are all generalities because every case is different. I try to approach each case on a case-by-case basis. But, generally, men view divorce as the ending of the marriage, and they are trying to split assets, and trying to minimize the amount of money the woman is going to get either through child support, spousal support, or the division of assets.

Women, on the other hand, view divorce as a way to start something new and to move on with their life. They're not really out to, in my opinion; maximize their divorce and the division of assets and the amount of support they get. I'm constantly telling women they should try to maximize those rights that the State of California and most states have given them. So, they kind of view divorce as a new start, and men view divorce as a way to make sure they're minimizing their financial exposure.

Interviewer: What are the most common reasons people give for why they want a divorce?

Vincent Davis: I think men give the reason that they've grown apart from their spouse. Generally, they may have found someone else that they feel is better suited.
Nowadays, I see a lot of women wanting to get divorced because the male is either, in their words, too controlling or there's been some type of domestic violence – either physical, verbal, or mental. Those are the main reasons why women want to get divorced. In my mind, when

listening to both sides, it's mainly because of a lack of, or a breakdown, in communication.

ATTORNEY'S APPEAL TO CLIENTS

Interviewer: Do you give people what they want or do you try to encourage them to go to counseling or work things out on their own?

Vincent Davis: I try to do all of the above, but many people come to me in different stages of either planning the divorce or thinking about divorce. About half of the clients that come to me for divorce have already filed divorce or already have an attorney that they're unhappy with.

Interviewer: What are some things that they're unhappy about?

Vincent Davis: Generally, they're unhappy with the attorney. They don't get the feeling that the attorney is giving them top-notch service. In my area, an average rate for an attorney would be anywhere from $250 to $350 an hour. For working class people, that's a lot of money. So if they feel that they're paying that amount of money, they want an attorney who is basically catering to their needs and returning their calls, responding to their emails, and performing well in court.

Maybe half of the people that come to me who already have attorneys realize, when they go to court, that their attorney is not a strong advocate. It's one thing to know about the family code, but it's another thing to be a trial attorney in court. That's a whole different skill; a lot of attorneys don't have the training or the experience to be a good trial lawyer.

I kind of have a unique background. For many years, I was on a court-appointed panel handling juvenile dependency cases, which is somewhat related to family law and divorce cases. I probably was in trial four out of the five days a week, if not every day, for almost 10 years. So, I have a lot of experience in being in trial every day, and then I also have the training that I received from Gerry Spence, who's probably viewed by most attorneys as the greatest trial attorney in American history.

COMMON MISCONCEPTIONS ABOUT DIVORCE

Interviewer: In California, do you need a valid reason to file for a divorce, or is California a no-fault state?

Vincent Davis: California is a no-fault state.

Interviewer: What are the most common misconceptions that people have about divorce that you have to dispel?

Vincent Davis: The most common misconception they have is that they can do it themselves.

I can't tell you how many clients come in to me after their divorce has been finalized, and they want me to try to fix something – a mistake that was made in their case that's now going to have a significant impact on them as they move forward in their life. Recently, I had a client who came in, and they went to a paralegal to  do all of the paperwork. It turns out that a mistake in the process is probably going to cost this particular client over $300,000. So,

sometimes clients are penny-wise and pound-foolish.

I always stress to clients, "Always go talk to a lawyer and try to get that free initial consultation, because that lawyer will tell you things that you just didn't know." I mean, the example I give a lot of times is, "If your doctor tells you, 'You need open heart surgery,' are you going to ask the doctor, 'Can I do it myself?' Absolutely not. But a lot of people feel that they can do their own divorce case themselves, or their own child custody case, or their own child support case.

How to Save Money on Your Divorce

Now, if they can't afford a lawyer, one of the things that we do is we represent people on what's called a "partial" or a "limited scope" basis. California allows attorneys to go in and represent clients for just one hearing, or in just one matter, or just one trial, or just for discovery. We do a lot of that work. Some clients can't even afford that, and we coach them, and we walk them through step-by-step on how to do their divorce.

One of the things that we started recently is a once-a-month seminar. For a nominal fee, that person can come to our seminar, get all of the forms they need to basically start and/or almost complete their divorce.

CaliforniaDivorceAttorney.co

TYPES & QUALITY OF REPRESENTATION

Interviewer: What are some of the disadvantages about those divorces for only $299 that people will see advertised, versus hiring a private lawyer?

Vincent Davis: Well, a $299 divorce is probably going to get you very, very little. Now, for some people, maybe that's all they need.

Because people sometimes agree, among themselves, how they're going to divide property. The classic case I get is a woman  comes in and says, "We've agreed upon everything. We just need you to write it up." I start writing it up, and then I realize that she's agreed to basically give away the farm. She didn't even know what rights she had to spousal support, to child support, or to half the husband's pension plan. So, in a $299 divorce, nobody's going to explain that to you. That's why you would at least want to go and speak to the private attorney for the free consultation. We give free consultations. Not all attorneys do. At least get an outline of your rights before you start. Then you can sit down with your spouse and try to work everything out for yourself.

I recently had a client who was about to agree to $1,500 a month in child support. We ran the numbers ourselves. We discovered the husband made so much money, that she was actually supposed to be receiving $6,000 in child support and spousal support per month. The difference between $6,000 and $1,500 multiplied by 12 months, multiplied by many years – that's a lot of money. Had she not been advised by a coworker to go talk to an attorney, she would've never known she was giving away so much money.

Interviewer: Is it wise to use just one attorney to negotiate the divorce, or does each person need their own separate attorney?

Vincent Davis: No. As a matter of fact, in California, that's probably against the law. You can't have an attorney representing both sides on a case, no matter what type of case, and especially a divorce. Nowadays, people are hiring family law attorneys to be mediators in their divorce. A mediator is not supposed to take any side with respect to whether certain rights are implemented or not.

So, I've done a couple of mediations. In those mediations, if an agreement is worked out, I tell the client, "You know what? I was your mediator. I was not the attorney for either of you. I didn't inform either of you of what the arguments or the rights would be sayain this matter." I try to clear this up right away. "That's not what my job was supposed to be. I think before you guys sign this agreement that you've mediated with me, you should go seek the advice of your own attorneys."

HOW TO CHOOSE A GOOD DIVORCE LAWYER

Interviewer: In your opinion. what makes a good divorce lawyer? What are some red flags a person should look out for when choosing a divorce lawyer?

Vincent Davis: I think there are probably three key areas that a person should look for when hiring a divorce attorney.

1. **The attorney must be a good listener.** If the attorney is not a good listener, that attorney will probably not proceed like the client wants or needs, and he'll probably not be a very good trial or in-court attorney because that attorney is not going to be listening to what the judge is saying.

2. **The attorney must be compassionate and understanding.** Typically, I hear the complaint about attorneys that we are not sympathetic enough to the client's plight. Sometimes, especially for people that are very experienced, they treat all divorces the same. At our office, we treat every case on a case-by-case basis and know every divorce is not the same.

3. **The attorney must be an experienced divorce lawyer.** Now, just because someone has passed the bar and has a law license doesn't mean s/he has experience. Someone recently asked me, "What medical school did your doctor graduate from? Where did

your doctor place or rank in medical school?" I was embarrassed to say that I didn't know the answers to those questions. The main reason why I didn't know the answers to those questions is because I was treating doctors as a commodity, as if they were all the same. I should have known better, because I know lawyers are not all the same. They vary in background, experience, knowledge, and just plain old abilities and training.

ALL ATTORNEYS ARE NOT THE SAME

Every lawyer is not the same. Every client should ask these questions their prospective attorney:

- How long have you been handling divorce cases?
- How many clients have you represented?
- How many actual divorce or family law <u>trials</u> have you done?

I know a lot of family law attorneys that have never been to trial. It's shocking – but true.

COMMUNICATION BETWEEN PARTIES

Interviewer: Once lawyers have been hired, are a husband and wife allowed to talk to each other, or does everything have to go through attorneys?

Vincent Davis: No. Husbands and wives are free to talk to each other any time they want. Whether that's a good idea or a bad idea is a whole separate question, but they are allowed to talk to each other any time.

MEDIATION V. COURT PROCESS

Interviewer: Let's talk about the mediation versus the court process. How do they differ?

Vincent Davis: Mediations are usually done with an experienced family law attorney or a retired judge. What people try to do is work out an agreement that they feel is fair to both sides.

Going to court is all about legal rights, about evidence, and about what the judge believes should be done. Judges aren't mediators. They decide contested issues of law and of fact.

Interviewer: When is mediation "better" than going to court, and when can it be worse?

Vincent Davis: Mediation is very good for people who have an idea of what their rights are to begin with, and they don't have to be educated. Maybe they have done some research on their own. It's also good for cases where there isn't a large family estate or a community property estate involved. Mediation is probably not as good when the parties don't actually know their rights and are relying upon friends and relatives or the other spouse to tell them what their rights are, or in cases where there's a high community property estate and there's a lot of money involved.

PLANNING AHEAD DURING DIVORCE

Interviewer: Should someone plan ahead when divorcing and figure out where they're going to live, what their budget will be, and things like that?

Vincent Davis: Yes. They should always plan. Getting the attorney involved at the earliest possible stage is the best idea. Someone said this recently: a lot of people plan more for their weddings than they do their divorce, and the divorce is probably way more important than the wedding ever was.

THE ISSUE OF CHILD CUSTODY

Interviewer: What happens when kids are involved? Does the mom automatically get full custody?

Vincent Davis: No, no. In California, both parties are entitled to have full custody, whether it's a father or a mother. I hear a lot of people say, "Well, judges always lean to the mother," and I don't find that true in my experience, especially nowadays. It's 2014. There are equal rights for both mothers and fathers.

Interviewer: The fact that a lot more women are working now these days. Do you think that's a contributing factor as well?

Vincent Davis: I do think so because you'd be surprised how many cases I've handled where the wife is the breadwinner, and the husband has the lower-paying job or, in a lot of cases, doesn't work at all.

Interviewer: How can custody battles be prevented or situations be made the best they could be? What's the best-case scenario? What's the best that a custody battle can be?

Vincent Davis: Well, custody battles can be prevented if both people are playing fair with each other and are mature about the raising of children. Unfortunately, the way California is set up, the person who has custody (or the most custody) gets a benefit with respect to the receipt or the paying of child support and spousal support. For example, the more custody or visitation you have (and if you're the higher income earner), the less child support you pay. Your decision about custody and visitation may be affected by the amount of money you could be required to pay the ex in child support and spousal support.

I've been involved in a lot of cases where the mother comes in, and we represent the mother, and she tells me, "You know, the dad hasn't been involved at all in the children's life for the past three years. I do everything. Now, all of a sudden, because he finds out he has to pay me a boatload of child support and spousal support, he wants to be the 50/50 caretaker of the child. But he works 60 hours a week, so how is that 50/50 custody even possible?"

Interviewer: How long is the custody process going to take, and what determines the division again?

Vincent Davis: In California, there is a standard called "best interests." If the parties can't agree, it's left to the judge to decide what is best for the child. There are many factors that the judge has to look at.

Interviewer: During cases that have foster children, how are those handled?

Vincent Davis: Foster children are handled, in California, in a completely different system. That's the Juvenile Dependency System, and there's nothing in the family law court that allows that to be dealt with.

OUT-OF-STATE COMPLICATIONS

Interviewer: What happens if one spouse

wants to move out of the state after the divorce or during it?

Vincent Davis: The spouse can always move any time they want. The problem becomes if they want to take the child with them.

Interviewer: What problems would they be facing there, and what would occur?

Vincent Davis: I have a case right now where the mother wants to move to London, England, and the father lives here and works here, and has substantial visitation with the child. The child is only three years old. What would happen to that relationship with the father if the mother moved to London, England? That's a long way away. It's not easy to have a two-hour drive, if that, across Los Angeles County to have your visitation. It's going to be very hurtful for the relationship of one of the parents if the other person's out-of-state, or even sometimes just out-of-county. I had a case recently where we represented the client in Los Angeles, and the parent wanted to move to San Francisco. It's an hour flight away, but that's still a long way if you want to see your child on a regular, frequent basis.

Interviewer: What are ways for people to go about if they wanted to relocate with the child? What's the process that someone needs to take if they want to relocate to another state or area with the child?

Vincent Davis: They either have to get one of two things: the agreement of the other parent or a court order.

There is a quite a procedure, in California, to get what's called a move-away order. It usually involves a custody and visitation evaluation by an outside psychiatrist or a psychologist who renders a report after interviewing both parents, the child, and other collateral witnesses to determine if moving away would be in the best interest of the child.

DIVISION OF ASSETS

Interviewer: How are assets and marital property divided in a divorce?

Vincent Davis: They're divided equally. That's the general rule. There may be some exceptions, but that's generally how they're divided.

Interviewer: What are some of the exceptions here? What about a property that belonged to maybe one person's family beforehand and now got inherited? Does that also become divided equally?

Vincent Davis: Inherited property generally is not divided between the spouses. It belongs to the spouse who inherited it, as his or her sole and separate property, unless that  spouse co-mingles or mixes that property or those assets with the community property.

Interviewer: What about a situation where the divorcing couple had a business together?

Vincent Davis: Then, the court has to come up with a fair distribution of the assets on a 50/50 basis. The trick is determining how much that business is worth. There are different ways that the court can do it. There's the book basis. There's the capital basis. There's the income basis. There's the future earnings basis.

This is where my financial expertise as a former Certified Public Accountant comes into play, because if you have a business that's really worth $1,000,000, but during the divorce that gets valued at $500,000, the spouse who's not going to keep the business is going to basically be cheated out of their half of $500,000, which is $250,000.

ALIMONY & CHILD SUPPORT

Interviewer: How does alimony work, and how is it calculated?

Vincent Davis: In California, it's called spousal support, and it's calculated based upon the income of both parties, the length of the  marriage, and the needs of both parties to continue on in the same lifestyle. There are two types of alimony or spousal support in California, and they're called temporary spousal support and permanent spousal support. They're computed a little bit differently, and they're based upon a few different factors.

Interviewer: What are some examples of those factors?

Vincent Davis: The primary difference is with the short-term or the temporary spousal support, which is usually put into place by a mathematical formula. A lot of attorneys and judges use something called DissoMaster (or XSpouse), which are computer programs to calculate the amount owed. That generally is the number that the court orders for child support. However, there are exceptions to this rule. You must confer with an experienced family law attorney to understand these exceptions.

In permanent spousal support, the court start with that number and either work their way up or down – usually it's down. There are a lot of other factors, like the ability to work. So, in a case where a mother or a wife hasn't been working, she got the DissoMaster amount. But, if the divorce pended, say, a year, that would've given her the ample opportunity to find a job, which would reduce the amount of spousal support that she would need.

Interviewer: How does child support work, and how is that calculated?

Vincent Davis: In California, child support is supposed to be, in 95% of the cases, a pure mathematical formula. They use

computing software programs like DissoMaster and Xspouse. What happens is you put certain numbers into a computer program, and out pops the amount for child support. There are numbers: for example, the amount of money that each person makes, their overtime, and their bonuses.

It takes into consideration taxes. It takes into consideration mortgages that are paid, health insurance, and who pays for those things. It takes into consideration whether somebody's paying child support for other children from another relationship. It takes into account how many children there are total. Just many, many, many factors are plugged into this computer program, and out pops a number that will give you the amount of what they call a guideline. In California, they call it "guideline child support."

Interviewer: What are some factors, other than the mathematical formula, that can be used in determining child support?

Vincent Davis: One of the classic ways of getting child support is to prove the actual need of the child. Let me give you an example. I currently represent someone who is a celebrity.

The computed guideline amount for child support was $24,000 per month. But, we were able to show the judge that the mother didn't need $24,000 per month so the court ordered a lower amount of child support which was $15,000 per month.

But, then the converse is true also. I've had cases where the mother has kept custody of the child. The guideline support was maybe $2,000 per month, but this child had special needs because of a disagnosis of autism. The mother actually needed more money to help take care of the child. So, there is a provision in California law that allows the judge to sometimes raise or lower that amount of child support based on need.

CHILD SUPPORT

Interviewer: For small children, are the costs of daycare and basic medical needs taken into consideration as well?

Vincent Davis: Yes, they are. Usually, the judge orders both people to provide insurance, or selects the parent whose employer provides medical insurance for dependents.

Interviewer: How long does one pay for child support?

Vincent Davis: Generally, until the child is 18.

Interviewer: Can child support get modified within that timeframe?

Vincent Davis: Yes. It can always be modified up or down, depending on changes in income of either party.

Interviewer: If the person had multiple children with that spouse, does the child support double or triple depending on the amount of children? Or, is it calculated in a certain way?

Vincent Davis: It's calculated in a certain way. It doesn't necessarily double or triple, but it increases significantly the more children that you have.

Interviewer: What if a spouse believes that the supported spouse is not using the alimony or child support money for the "right" things?

Vincent Davis: He/she can go back to court and try to modify it downward. That is a difficult thing to do in California, but it can be done.

ADVICE TO CLIENTS

Interviewer: What are some more tips that you have to help people get through a divorce without destroying their life, their ex-spouse's life, and their children's lives?

Vincent Davis: The biggest tip that I can say, and I recommend this to a lot of people, but unfortunately you need the agreement of the other spouse, is probably go to marital counseling. Even if you're breaking up and you've decided you're going to get divorced, at least learn how to deal with each other in a civil manner. So much money is burned up in divorces when people are represented by attorneys, and it's not the attorneys burning up the money. It's the feuding spouses who are burning up the money. I was recently involved in a case a few years ago where they were fighting about a family pet.

In California, pets, although near and dear to everyone's heart, are treated as property. So, they were arguing and spent a lot of money about who was going to get the family pet.

But, the problem with divorces is a lot of the egos and emotions get involved. That drives people, unfortunately, to fight more. This is a very, very delicate situation. An attorney is telling a client, "It may be in your best interest to try to resolve these issues or to try to mediate some of these issues." Those attorneys, in a lot of cases, end up getting fired, and the feuding spouses go find another attorney who's going to kick butt and take names. So, it's a very, very delicate situation, because at the time, these spouses are only seeing fire. They're only seeing red, and they don't care what's reasonable.

So, the best thing I would advise is no matter what, no matter how your ex-spouse pushes your buttons, to try to step back and try to look at this calmly and collectedly. I tell a lot of my clients, "If you've made a decision that you're not going to get back with that person, and you've really made that decision in your heart, don't talk to the person anymore. Do things over email. Do things through your attorney. Do things via text."

That's because, if a person has known you many, many years, they are going to know how to push your buttons. So, when your buttons are pushed, you see red. You see anger, and ego, and jealousy, and all of those emotions get in the way. What happens is you end up fighting over something that's really not important, and then two years down the road, the spouses scratch their heads and say, "Why were we fighting so much, and why did the lawyers get all of the money?"

CLIENT EMOTIONALITY DURING A DIVORCE

Interviewer: How do you usually help remove the emotional aspects of your client's case?

Vincent Davis: Oh, I don't try to. I try to just listen to my clients. I'm a pretty calm guy, and so hopefully my clients, at some point in time, start to mirror the way that I approach the case. I try to lead by example, in other words.

CHALLENGES OF DIVORCE CASES

Interviewer: What would you say are some of the more challenging aspects of a divorce case?

Vincent Davis: For me, it's trying to explain things to the client, because a lot of times, people get advice from their friends, their coworkers, and their relatives. Sometimes, that advice is just 100% incorrect. They come to you thinking that it's the gospel. So, it's trying to explain to clients and control expectations.

The hardest thing for the client, probably, is to learn that the law is not what they thought it was and to accept that.

DIVORCE PROCESS TIMELINE

Interviewer: When a client meets with you for the first time, in your experience, what have you observed are some of the common things that they ask?

Vincent Davis: The most common thing that I get asked is, "How fast can I be divorced?"

Interviewer: How long could a divorce case potentially last?

Vincent Davis: They last anywhere from a couple days to two or three years.

Interviewer: What's the order of the way things are handled in a divorce? From my understanding, there's a mediation process. What gets decided first? If there are children involved, is it custody? Then, does it go to the division of assets? What's the order that you usually do it in?

Vincent Davis: That's all dependent upon the attorney and the strategy. There is no particular order.

PRENUPTIAL AGREEMENTS

Interviewer: What is a prenuptial agreement, and how does that come into play during a divorce?

Vincent Davis: Pre- and postnuptial agreements are basically contracts, between the spouses, to limit

certain types of distributions of assets or support at the end of the marriage. One of the first things that happens in California is that you have to find out if the pre- or postnuptial agreement was done fairly, and if it complied with certain rules and regulations.

Interviewer: What are some of the more common misconceptions people have about prenups?

Vincent Davis: That they're 100% valid.

COMMON LAW AND SAME-SEX MARRIAGE

Interviewer: What about common law marriages in California? Is that existent? How does that work?

Vincent Davis: Non-existent.

Interviewer: Is there anything similar to common law marriages in California that work similar to actual marriages?

Vincent Davis: No.

Interviewer: What about same-sex marriages?

Vincent Davis: Yes. There are same-sex marriages currently in California. I want to stress that: "currently." I don't make any judgment one way or the other, but, yes, we do now have same-sex marriages.

Interviewer: Now, are divorce proceedings handled similarly or are there any differences with same-sex marriages?

Vincent Davis: Currently, they're handled similarly.

ANNULMENT IN THE STATE OF CALIFORNIA

Interviewer: Does annulment ever come into play at any point?

Vincent Davis: Yes. In California, you can file for an annulment.

Interviewer: What's the difference between an annulment and a divorce?

Vincent Davis: Annulment is to declare that the marriage never existed.

Divorce is, "We were married. Now, we're getting divorced, and we're going to talk about custody of the children, and we're going to talk about division of the assets."

Annulment is, "There was a marriage, but it was void, meaning illegal as a matter of law. Therefore, we don't have to divide anything. It's just as if it never happened."

It used to come up a lot in terms of religion when, for example, if you were Catholic, you couldn't get remarried. Well, you weren't supposed to get remarried unless you'd had an annulment.

Interviewer: Does the annulment have an additional cost?

Vincent Davis: Additional to a divorce? No. It's handled just like a divorce case.

UNCONTESTED VS. CONTESTED DIVORCE

Interviewer: What would be the definition or the difference between an uncontested versus a contested divorce?

Vincent Davis: Uncontested is usually, "Hey. We've agreed upon everything, and there is no dispute. We have a settlement agreement." Or, where one party is served and doesn't show up in court, and the party doing the serving can get whatever they want through an uncontested hearing. Contested means there are disputes between both parties regarding the law and/or fact, and they need a judge to make those decisions for them.

PATERNITY CASES & RESTRAINING ORDERS

Interviewer: What about cases where, let's say, the couple isn't married, yet they have children together?

Vincent Davis: Those are called paternity cases.

Interviewer: How do those work as far as custody and time-sharing? Would you say it's similar to an actual divorce proceeding?

Vincent Davis: No, no. Well, it's a divorce proceeding, but the only issues are custody, visitation, and support, and sometimes restraining orders.

RESTRAINING ORDERS (TRO)

Interviewer: How would restraining orders come into play? How do those work, and what are some of the key factors that people need to be aware of when it comes to restraining orders?

Vincent Davis: Try not to get yourself in the situation of having a restraining order; try not to get yourself in the situation of violating a restraining order. If you do need a restraining order, or to defend against a restraining order, it's imperative that you speak to an attorney, even if it's a free consultation, because there could be criminal ramifications.

CONCLUSION

If you are located in California, please call our toll-free number for a consultation.

(888) 888-6582

We can provide services to you in various ways:

1. **Full legal representation including**
   a. Preparation of all documents and forms
   b. Preparing and responding to all formal and informal discovery.
   c. Representing you at all court hearings and trials.
2. **Limited-Scope Representation** (Bundled Services)

a. We represent you on a flat-fee basis for:
    i. Document and form preparation
    ii. PPreparing and/or responding to discovery
    iii. Representing you at a hearing or trial
3. Our monthly seminars where we can show you how to do it yourself
    a. These seminars will soon be available online.
4. In person, Telephone or Scope of Case An Analysis
    a. We sit with you and assist you with your case; and/or assist you in helping your attorney.

DISCLAIMER

This publication is intended to be informational only.
No legal advice is being given, and no attorney-client relationship is intended to be created by reading this material. If you are facing legal issues, whether criminal or civil, seek professional legal counsel to get your questions answered.

Law Offices of Vincent W. Davis & Associates

150 N. Santa Anita Ave., Ste. 200
Arcadia, CA 91006

(888) 888-6582

Offices in:

Arcadia	Beverly Hills	Irvine
La Mirada	Long Beach	Los Angeles
Ontario	Riverside	Woodland Hills

www.VincentWDavis.com

Made in the USA
Columbia, SC
11 April 2019